Up Close & Personal Vanessa Hudgens
THE UNAUTHORIZED BIOGRAPHY

Grace Norwich

PUFFIN

PUFFIN BOOKS

Published by the Penguin Group: London, New York, Australia, Canada, India,
Ireland, New Zealand and South Africa
Penguin Books Ltd, Registered Offices: 80 Strand, London WC2R 0RL, England

puffinbooks.com

First published in the United States of America as *Vanessa Hudgens: Breaking Free –
An Unauthorized Biography* by Price Stern Sloan, a division of Penguin Young
Readers Group, Penguin Group (USA) Inc., 2007
Published in Great Britain in Puffin Books 2008
1

The website links in this book are to third-party Internet websites which are
controlled and maintained by others. These links are included solely for the
convenience of readers and do not constitute any endorsement by Penguin Books
Limited ('Penguin') of the sites linked or referred to, nor does Penguin have any
control over or responsibility for the content of any such sites.

Made and printed in England by Clays Ltd, St Ives plc

British Library Cataloguing in Publication Data
A CIP catalogue record for this book is available from the British Library

ISBN: 978-0-141-32575-0

www.greenpenguin.co.uk

Penguin Books is committed to a sustainable future
for our business, our readers and our planet.
The book in your hands is made from paper
certified by the Forest Stewardship Council.

contents

introduction

Into the Spotlight

Sometimes art really does imitate life. Just look at Vanessa Anne Hudgens. In the smash-hit movie *High School Musical*, the diminutive, dark-haired beauty plays the part of Gabriella, a shy brainiac who ends up sharing the spotlight with the most popular guy in school. It's your classic geek-to-chic success story. In real life, Vanessa may not have been a geek growing up, but she definitely wasn't the centre of attention. Far from it! 'I personally have moved a lot in my life,' the nineteen-year-old California native told *Life Story* magazine, 'so I don't really have much in the way of friends. Because I keep moving and moving and moving, it's hard for me to keep friends and just live a normal life.' Since she lived in many different places, Vanessa was actually taught at home by her mother. So it's not that she wasn't the most popular girl in school. She wasn't in school to begin with!

But just like Gabriella, who bravely takes the microphone during the karaoke scene at the opening of *HSM*, Vanessa decided that she was going to be someone that people noticed and looked up to. And just like Gabriella, she decided to use her amazing singing and dancing skills to catapult herself into the spotlight. Of course, fame and fortune don't just happen overnight. For Vanessa, the path to stardom would span almost a decade. There were the many small roles in local theatres starting at the age of eight, the countless commercial auditions, the bit parts on television, the first big screen opportunity, and of course, her breakout performance in *HSM*.

Obviously, Vanessa has tons of talent, but to make it in the demanding, and at times cut-throat, entertainment industry, you need a lot of support at home. Fortunately, Vanessa gets plenty of that as well. 'They are good advice-givers,' she said of her parents in an interview with *Scholastic News Online*. 'Whenever I have a problem they are always there for me, [encouraging me] to never give up on something I really believe in.' We don't learn much about Gabriella's home life in *HSM*, but chances are it's a pretty healthy, nurturing environment as well.

As good as everything turns out for Gabriella at the make-believe East High School, that's nothing compared to the real-life success that Vanessa is enjoying. Two of her closest friends are Ashley Tisdale and Zac Efron. (There are even rumours that Vanessa and Zac are more than just friends, but more on that later!) As for music, Vanessa isn't just dabbling in a career. She's been on tour with the likes of The Cheetah Girls, one of America's hottest bands. Then there's her solo album, which could just make Vanessa as big as Kelly Clarkson or Jessica Simpson.

There's one last thing that Vanessa shares with Gabriella: a future. The Disney Channel has already released a sequel and they're busy getting ready for *HSM 3* to hit the big screens in 2008. The network executives are keeping a pretty tight lid on the plotline, but one thing is certain: we're going to see a lot more of Gabriella – as well as Troy, Sharpay and the rest of the gang from East High. More Gabriella of course means more Vanessa. But this is where art stops imitating life. Whereas Gabriella exists only in the world of *High School Musical*, Vanessa has a life outside of the movie. And what a life it is, as you're about to discover!

chapter 1
An American Girl

Vanessa Hudgens was born on 14 December 1988, in Salinas, California. On her birth certificate, Vanessa's parents, Greg and Gina, gave their firstborn the middle name Anne, which a lot of fans still know her by. But Vanessa actually decided to drop Anne from her name when she launched her solo music career. More on that later – right now in the story, Vanessa hasn't even said her first word, let alone burst out into song!

Though the Hudgens family would end up moving around a lot, Vanessa's early years were spent in sunny Salinas. By all accounts, this small city located between San Francisco and Los Angeles is a pretty awesome place to grow up. If nothing else, there's tons of healthy, delicious food there. In fact, Salinas is known as 'The Salad Bowl of the World' because it produces so many fresh vegetables, including lettuce, mushrooms, broccoli and artichokes. (Vanessa loves fresh veggies, except for carrots. She can't even stand the sight of one.) Next time you order a salad in a restaurant in America, chances are it started in the same place as Vanessa!

Of course, there's more to do in Salinas than pick and eat vegetables. The ocean is less than ten miles away and there are the nearby Sierra Mountains, which offer all sorts of winter activities, from skiing to snowboarding.

Vanessa's father is a busy firefighter, so the Hudgens household was a very active place. The arrival of baby Vanessa only added to the excitement. The energy she brings to her acting and music performances (not to mention the bubbly effervescence she injects into every interview) was clearly there from the very beginning. 'I started dancing at three,' Vanessa admitted to *The Dallas Morning News*. That must have been a toddler with serious moves!

Besides being an energetic baby, Vanessa was

surely one of the cutest around. Her father is Irish and Native American while her mother is Filipino, Chinese and Spanish. All the very best physical traits of those different ethnicities came together in Vanessa. Just look at her beautiful brown eyes, her long and lustrous dark hair, her big, bright smile and her perfect olive complexion.

You could argue that Vanessa's mixed background makes her one of the most all-American performers of her generation. After all, the United States is all about diversity, with people from all over the world living there. Vanessa truly embodies that multicultural spirit. This is something that she recognizes and embraces. 'I see myself as American,' she said in a conversation with *Life Story* magazine. 'I try to speak Filipino, but it's just so funny because I mangle it.' In the same interview, she admitted, 'I've come to see myself as a chameleon because I almost blend in with other people.' Vanessa represents the true American melting pot.

Vanessa's ability to step into another person's shoes is probably what got her interested in acting. In any event, the dancing she'd been doing since the age of three couldn't keep her entertained. The stage was calling! 'I started [musical theatre] when I was, like, seven,' Vanessa told USNews.com. 'I'll love it until the dying day!'

By this time, the Hudgens family had moved to San Diego, a larger California city just a few miles from the Mexican border. Some kids hate the idea of moving around, but Vanessa has always been able to manage it. This might have something to do with her star sign: Sagittarius. You may not totally believe in astrology, but in Vanessa's case, some of the information is revealing. Maybe the most telling tidbit is the fact that Sagittarians love to move around. Travel and exploration rank high on their list of likes. (Interestingly, the name 'Vanessa' was coined by the eighteenth-century writer Jonathan Swift who wrote the novel *Gulliver's Travels*, which, as the title suggests, also deals with themes of travel and exploration.) In addition to being full of wanderlust, Sagittarians are also very vibrant and energetic, qualities that definitely describe Vanessa.

Whether it has to do with astrology or simply the

fact that her home life was so healthy and stable, Vanessa was able to make a smooth transition to San Diego. Besides a new house, Vanessa had something else to get used to: a new baby sister. The littlest of the Hudgens clan was named Stella.

Vanessa took to the part of big sis right away and has never got bored with it. In fact, she's been the perfect role model for Stella, who is seven years younger. '[Stella] is my mini-me,' Vanessa told *Life Story* magazine. 'We listen to the same music, we dress the same – sometimes she's even way more fashionable than me and I end up saying, "I have to go change now, because you look too good." She's just so much fun.' All big sisters should be so supportive! (It's paid off too, with Stella enjoying her own success as a performer. She's been in a bunch of television commercials and has even appeared on some shows, including *According to Jim*.)

With two high-energy girls running around, the Hudgens household was definitely a theatrical place. The sisters' grandparents were all musicians, so the need to perform is clearly in their blood. But Vanessa was anxious to get up in front of people other than her little sister. San Diego is a far cry from Hollywood, so the only realistic outlet for Vanessa's passion to perform was community theatre. Even at the tender age of seven, she approached it with the energy and courage of a serious professional. Directors took notice, and Vanessa was soon landing parts in all sorts of musicals. In just a few short years, her résumé already included parts in such performances as *Evita*, *Carousel*, *The Wizard of Oz*, *The King and I*, *The Music Man*, *Cinderella* and *Damn Yankees*. Those are the canon of musical theatre, classic shows that gave Vanessa a great foundation for future acting.

Vanessa loved being up on the stage, and many of the performers she admires the most are known for their work in musicals. For instance, she's totally flattered when fans compare her to Olivia Newton John, who was immortalized for her portrayal of Sandy in the hit movie musical *Grease*. 'I love her!' Vanessa gushed in the *Atlanta Journal-Constitution*.

Still, as much as she enjoyed doing community theatre, Vanessa felt a strong pull to work in television and movies. Not that she was all about performing. As we've already seen, Vanessa is really into family, so a lot of her time was spent just hanging out at home. She told TV.com that her favourite sound in the entire world is her mother's laugh. How sweet is that?

Gina Hudgens has clearly been a huge influence in both of her daughters' lives, so much so that she eventually ended up teaching them at home. As Vanessa revealed in *Life Story* magazine, 'There's a part of me that wants to be the teen prom queen, but I've never gone to regular high school because I've been homeschooled since I was in eighth grade.'

Homeschooling, as the practice is known, used to be really rare, but it's becoming more and more common. There are more than a million kids in the United States who are schooled at home! There are many different reasons kids are homeschooled, from religion to geography to a side career, which was the case with Vanessa. It's just one more way that Vanessa really embodies the modern American teen. And contrary to what some people think, homeschooling doesn't make it hard to make friends. 'Oh, no, I'm friends with everybody,' Vanessa said in an interview to JustJared.com. 'I'm pretty much living the American lifestyle.'

When Vanessa did attend school with other kids, she enjoyed the experience, although regular school was not without its embarrassing moments. One time she got caught passing a note to her fifth-grade boyfriend, Sean. '[The teacher] took it and read the note in front of the class,' Vanessa told *Bop* magazine. 'OMG, I almost died!' So what was in the note, anyway? 'The note was sweet,' she said. 'It was before summer break and I wrote, "I'll miss you." It was still embarrassing though!'

With Mom at the head of the class, note passing became an activity of the past. Not that Vanessa minded. Studies were always more important than socializing for young Vanessa. Much like Gabriella, the character she would play in *High School Musical*, Vanessa favoured science class. In fact, she actually envisioned a career in the sciences. 'I used to always want to be a pediatrician, because I love kids,' she told *Life Story* magazine. Of course, that was just one of Vanessa's career ambitions. She continues: 'I came across an autobiography I wrote on myself in the fifth grade, and I wrote, "When I get older, I want to be a movie star or a pediatrician." ' Both are good choices!

It could have gone either way for Vanessa: science or stardom. But then fate intervened. Vanessa's big break came when a friend, also a performer, had to skip an audition for a television commercial. She suggested Vanessa go in her place. Always positive, Vanessa jumped at the opportunity. And of course, she nailed the audition! With that one foot in the door of the entertainment industry, Vanessa's career was off and running.

chapter 2

Break Out on the Big Screen

With Vanessa's passion for acting, great attitude, supportive family and, well, gorgeous looks, it seemed only a matter of time before she landed something substantial in the way of a meaty role. Not that she wasn't happy with her musical theatre and commercials, but hey, what actress wouldn't want to be in a film with an Oscar-winning actress that is so controversial it gets just about everybody's attention?

Well, Vanessa landed a part in just such a film called *Thirteen*, which hit the cinemas to millions of shocked parents on 20 August 2003. If you're thinking *Thirteen* relates to an unlucky number or some horror movie with spooky stuff and lots of blood and gore, you couldn't be more wrong. Not that the film wasn't scary. *Thirteen* really earned its 18 rating in categories like violence, drug use, sexuality and bad language. Vanessa describes the film this way: 'It was basically about wild teenagers who make the wrong decisions and take the wrong path,' she told *Life Story*. 'When kids are young they want to experience things, but they don't see what the downside to it is. All they see is, "Oh, we're going to be crazy and do stupid stuff." '

And, boy, do the kids in this film go crazy. In this tortured mother-daughter tale, a seventh-grader named Tracy from the San Fernando Valley goes through a troubling transformation from a sweet, responsible student to an out-of-control mess. The whole sad story starts when thirteen-year-old Tracy (played by Evan Rachel Wood) wants to get in with the 'cool' crowd. And that means a whole lot of lying to her mother, Mel, played by the amazing Oscar-winning actress Holly Hunter. Tracy's brother in *Thirteen* is played by Brady Corbet, whom Vanessa would soon work with again. So the name *Thirteen* refers to Tracy's volatile age. The film depicts the harsher side of middle school when Tracy begins to shoplift, hang around with boys she hardly knows, and do other self-destructive things like taking drugs and drinking.

It's kind of funny that Vanessa's first film was one that her mom probably would never let her go see if she weren't already in it! A lot of people were really troubled by the movie because it was so realistic in its portrayal of kids trying to become adults too quickly. The reason for that is because the edgy flick was co-written by a real thirteen-year-old! It's incredible, but true.

Nikki Reed wrote the script with first-time director Catherine Hardwicke while she was going through her own teenage angst. In fact, the film is based on her own life. Catherine met and became friends with Nikki when she started dating the girl's divorced father. When she noticed that Nikki was going through some super-hard times, Catherine suggested she write her life experiences down as a way to put some of the negativity behind her. Those thoughts ended up becoming the project of a lifetime. Talk about taking something bad and turning it into something good!

Even though it was a first for both (Nikki had never written a script, and Catherine, who had been a production designer, had never directed), they ended up with a film that garnered a lot of attention and awards for the honest way it described the difficulties of growing up. Being a teenager has never been easy, but with all the crazy things happening in the world today, it's harder than ever. Catherine wanted to give viewers the feeling of this frenetic time. So she mostly used a handheld Super 16 camera to shoot her film, which gave the movie a look as erratic as its main subject. For an hour and thirty-five minutes, viewers watch shaky scenes that escalate in tension as Tracy and Mel clash over a six-month time span.

Nikki also ended up snagging herself a part (hey, she did write the script after all). The dark-haired writer played the part of Evie Zamora, the friend Tracy tries to win over by doing so many bad things. It's Evie who introduces Tracy to a cornucopia of rebellion: body piercing, shoplifting, drugs and reckless sexual behaviour. Evie is one bad seed, and she's the most popular girl in school. Yikes!

Part of Tracy's entrance into Evie's exclusive (and mean) clique means getting rid of her old friends. And that's where Vanessa's part comes in. No, Vanessa didn't play one of the bad girls skipping school and stuffing stolen clothes into her bag. The casting agents couldn't get past her sweet smile when figuring out her role. In her first film, she played Noel, one of Tracy's old friends from when the thirteen-year-old was still a top student and a normal kid. But unfortunately for Noel (or maybe fortunately, depending on how you look at it), Tracy has to ditch her in order to shed her innocent image. Ditch Vanessa? That's nuts!

Thirteen was a serious educational experience for Vanessa, and not just in filmmaking or acting. Because of her childhood – growing up in the business and generally not being around a lot of her peers since she didn't attend normal school – Vanessa wasn't familiar with the problems of peer pressure. The most pressure Vanessa ever had was when her little sister, Stella, begged to borrow her clothes. 'When I did that movie, I had no idea what they were talking about,' she told *Life Story*. 'I was more sheltered from things, but the movie definitely woke me up to what a crazy world it is and what's out there and what kids sometimes do. There are so many other paths they can take.'

The role was a big leap for the star Evan Rachel Wood, best known at the time for her role as Jessie Sammler on the hit ABC drama *Once and Again*, which was about two divorced parents who begin a new life together. The characters on that show had family problems, but nothing compared to those in *Thirteen*. Despite her lack of experience with such gritty material, Evan received praise from critics for her performance of a teen in turmoil.

You have to give credit to these young actors who offer a candid view of how peers can affect a kid for good or for bad. Vanessa certainly felt the movie had a serious point to make. 'People really need to be educated about things like drugs and alcohol and what they can do to you in the long term,' she told *Life Story*. She knows what lesson she took away from the film. 'You just shouldn't do it, and it's not something that's very beneficial to you in the first place. Go out and shop if that makes you feel better, rather than doing something stupid or that you're pressured into doing.'

The critics commended not only the young actors but also the adults involved in this picture. Holly Hunter, who has racked up a lot of awards in her career, was nominated for the 2003 Academy Award for Best Actress in a Supporting Role. Not bad, but it doesn't end there. Both Holly and Evan were nominated for Golden Globes that same year: Holly was up for Best Supporting Actress, and Evan for Best Actress in a Drama.

Vanessa's rewards were more reflective. She saw how destructive drugs, crime and peer pressure can become and vowed to be her own person no matter what others say. As she explained to *Life Story*, 'Being cool is being your own self, not doing something that someone else is telling you to do.'

chapter 3
Just One of the Guys

After she landed her first film part in a successful movie about the woes of adolescence, Vanessa immediately took her career in the completely opposite direction. Her next movie couldn't have been more different than the boundary-pushing *Thirteen*. Vanessa was cast in *Thunderbirds*, a live-action remake of the 1960s futuristic TV series that had been done entirely with puppets. Despite its description, Vanessa's next project wasn't all fun and games. The colourful, lighthearted movie would have its own challenges. The young actress would have to travel far from home, since *Thunderbirds* was filmed in the UK and the Seychelles. But it was worth it.

Originally, *Thunderbirds* was a British television show that revolved around the extraordinary life of the

Tracy family – whose members made up the crisis-solving International Rescue team. Using 'supermarionation' puppetry, the show was a cult hit that spread to countries across the globe, including Canada, Australia, the United States, New Zealand and Japan. In the original series, all the action was done with miniatures made by Derek Meddings, who later won an Oscar for his special effects on the film *Superman*.

Thunderbirds starts in the year 2065, with the Tracy clan busy saving people from disasters with the use of high-tech rockets and vehicles. The head of the family is ex-astronaut and widowed millionaire Jeff Tracy (played by Bill Paxton) who employs all of his sons in his heroics – all, that is, except for the youngest son, Alan. The youngest Tracy son is played by none other than Brady Corbet, who also appeared as the older brother in *Thirteen*.

Brady's character, Alan, is still in boarding school and feels left out since the rest of his family have a lot of adventures. But when Alan is on holiday from school and at the unmapped secret island in the South Pacific that the Tracys call home, the rest of his family gets stuck in outer space (it sounds crazy, but, hey, it's a sci-fi style adventure flick). So when master villain The Hood – played by the top-notch actor Ben Kingsley – tries to use the Thunderbirds' special machines to rob banks all over the world, the only family member around to save the day is Alan. Enter Vanessa. She plays Tin-Tin, an adventurous and loyal pal who is one of Alan's best friends. Alan's other closest friend is the nerdy and nervous Fermat played by the adorable Soren Fulton. Together, the three of them take care of business while the other Tracys are in space.

Turning this quirky, British cult hit into a massive American movie with real actors and real action wouldn't be easy. Universal Pictures sunk seventy million dollars into the effort. For Vanessa, this was a tremendous leap. *Thirteen* had a tiny budget like most independent films – less than two million dollars. For *Thunderbirds*, the studio needed a director passionate about sci-fi and action-fantasy movies. Jonathan Frakes fitted the bill. He had directed a few Star Trek films – *Star Trek: First Contact* and *Star Trek: Insurrection* – as well as the action hit *Clockstoppers*. To add to his sci-fi résumé, Jonathan also played Commander Riker on *Star Trek: The Next Generation*. Others enlisted in the project were screenwriters Michael McCullers (who penned the hilarious Austin Powers flicks) and William Osborne (who wrote *The Scorpion King*).

From the plot description, *Thunderbirds* might sound like something to take your little brother or sister to see, but director Jonathan Frakes argued that this wasn't a movie for tykes. 'I don't think this is a kids' movie,' he told *CanWest News Service*. 'It happens to star three great young adults.' That's right, he's talking about Brady, Vanessa and Soren.

Brady, who was fifteen at the time, had eagerly signed up to play the role of Alan. Born in Scottsdale, Arizona, Brady made his feature film debut in *Thirteen* just like Vanessa. But he had a lot of TV roles before that, including guest appearances on *The King of Queens*, *Greetings from Tucson* and *Oliver Beene*. Brady got his start in acting at the age of seven, when he landed his first commercial.

He knew *Thunderbirds* from watching reruns late at night on cable TV. 'I don't sleep very much, and it comes on at like three a.m.,' he told *CanWest News Service*. 'So it was always on my periphery.' He wasn't disappointed by his decision. Jonathan Frakes filled *Thunderbirds* with super high-tech vehicles such as the Thunderbird 1: a high-speed rocket that hit fifteen thousand miles per hour. Or if that isn't cool enough, Thunderbird 4 turns into a mini-submarine. '[Production designer] John Beard has created the most fantastic bold world,' Brady said [to *CanWest*]. 'Everything is in primary colours. It's big and bright, and almost like something out of a comic book.' That fantastic world Brady describes includes couches in the shape of bananas, and coffee tables that look like orange peanuts.

While making a movie where you lounge on big bananas and ride mini submarines might seem like fun, it's actually hard, hard work. A lot of the acting took place in front of a green screen and nothing else. A computer later filled in all the villains and sci-fi threats. So the actors really had to use their imaginations to paint the picture around them as they did their scenes.

The director talked to Vanessa, Brady and Soren in advance about what would be filled in later. 'We developed a lot of what the movie was going to look like in preproduction, so I was able to share with these guys what (for example) they would be seeing out the window of the spaceship,' Jonathan Frakes told *CanWest*. 'The visual effects team would also come to rehearsals and when we were preparing to shoot.' Still, the burden rested mainly with the young actors, who had to translate those visions into expressions on their faces and appropriate physical movements.

Soren loved the challenge. 'It wasn't hard for me because I've got a really big imagination,' he said to *CanWest*. 'It's like a bubble inside my head, one of those thought bubbles where you're picturing everything.' Soren also started acting early, at the age of eight. By the time he landed *Thunderbirds*, he was a film pro, having appeared in many movies including *Face to Face*, *Van Wilder* and *A Ring of Endless Light*. His TV credits are even more impressive. Soren's soulful eyes and shy smile landed him guest spots on *George Lopez*, *Crossing Jordan*, *Frasier*, *Charmed* and *Mad TV*.

In addition to acting against a green screen and fighting super-villains in locations halfway across the world, Vanessa had another challenge. She was basically surrounded by guys 24/7. Oh, poor thing, she had to put up with gorgeous Brady and sweet Soren. But seriously, it could be intimidating as the only girl on set. But not for our brave Vanessa, who hardly noticed she was the odd man, or rather woman, out. 'I seriously look at them as my friends,' she told *CanWest*. 'Soren and I got really close.' Jonathan backs up his favourite young actress. 'Vanessa was one of the guys, in the story and out,' he told *CanWest*. 'She would try anything I would ask her to try. I must say all my talent were really up for it.'

The three young actors gave *Thunderbirds* their all, but unfortunately that wasn't good enough. When it made its world premiere on 8 May 2004, at the Tribeca Film Festival, *Thunderbirds* was far from a critical success. Unlike *Thirteen*, some people found the film bland and unimportant. Famed film critic Roger Ebert gave it a big thumbs down. 'A movie like this is harmless, I suppose,' he said. 'But as an entertainment, it sends the kids tiptoeing through the multiplex to sneak into *Spider-Man 2*.'

In the *Sacramento Bee*, Joe Baltake got really harsh: 'Apologies to Gerry and Sylvia Anderson, creators of that singularly funky '60s marionette TV series *Thunderbirds*, for the way big Hollywood money has mangled their material for the new Universal film version.' Jay Boyar of the *Orlando Sentinel* called the film a stinker, writing: 'As the film is ending, you feel like shouting Thunderbirds are gone!'

But Vanessa still got respect for her part. In Australia's *Sunday Tasmanian*, writer Stuart Diwell describes Vanessa as 'impressive as the take-charge Tin-Tin'. So what if she had one flop? Vanessa seemed poised to become a bona fide movie actress. But something was about to get in the way.

chapter 4

Small Screen Successes

It used to be that actors ultimately aspired to star in movies. But these days, TV is where it's at. In school halls, kids talk excitedly about the latest episodes of their favourite television shows. Office workers gab about TV at the watercooler. Once or twice a year, a film breaks out and makes a splash during its opening weekend. But more often than not, viewers leave the cinema disappointed with a movie's expensive but dull results. With more big stars and famous writers flocking to television, the medium has captured the popular imagination of the American people. Vanessa, our favourite small star, couldn't resist the small screen, which beckoned with versatile characters on a wide range of shows.

Television is not easy to make. The whole process of getting an idea made into a show and then on to a cable channel or network is a mega rollercoaster ride. The first step involves producers and writers, who pitch their ideas to executives in the hopes that they will get money to make a pilot, which is a sample show. Then once the pilot is made, the producers watch it to see if it merits a series and a shot on television. But even if it passes that phase and gets on TV, a show can be pulled at any minute if viewers don't tune in. All the while, actors who get cast in these pilots and shows are biting their nails, hoping that they are part of the rare TV smash hit.

For a young actress as cute and talented as Vanessa, television provided a lot of chances to work, even if most of them were short-lived. It's no surprise that once she went out on auditions, producers quickly cast her in their shows. In 2002, she landed a guest appearance on the CBS drama *Robbery Homicide Division*, about an elite group of LA detectives, and starring veteran actor Tom Sizemore.

That same year, she got a small part on another CBS show called *Still Standing*. This one was relatively new

(Vanessa appeared on only the fourth episode called 'Still Rocking') and it was a comedy. Created by Diane Burroughs and Joey Gutierrez, this long-running CBS sitcom revolved around Bill and Judy Miller, high-school sweethearts who have to suffer seriously unglamourous jobs (toilet salesman and dental assistant) while raising a family of three in Chicago. Still, Bill and Judy haven't given up trying to be cool parents. Judy is played by Jami Gertz – a talented actress who rose to fame in the 1980s and appeared in such hit TV shows as *ER*, *Ally McBeal* and *The Facts of Life*. British-born Mark Addy is Bill Miller. Addy starred in the hit 1997 film *The Full Monty*, about six unemployed steel workers who create a male striptease act, despite the fact that they're not the hottest guys in the world. Vanessa was lucky to work with such seasoned pros.

It didn't end there. The roles kept rolling in. The following year, Vanessa scored a guest role as Lindsey on the Nickelodeon show *The Brothers Garcia*, on the episode called 'New Tunes', which aired in July of 2003. Directed by real-life brothers Gibby and Mike Cevallos,

The Brothers Garcia told the story of a Mexican-American family in San Antonio, Texas, and all the comic things that happened in their everyday lives. *Brothers*, which ran from 2000 to 2003, scored the highest ratings of any Nickelodeon show since 1996.

Comedy was definitely a good fit for Vanessa, and she had guest appearances on a lot of sitcoms, including *Quintuplets* on Fox. On this show – created by Mark Reisman, one of the masterminds behind the longstanding hit *Frasier* – comedian Andy Richter is Bob Chase, the father of, you guessed it, quintuplets. He and his wife, Carol (Rebecca Creskoff), try to raise five fifteen-year-olds in a three-bedroom home. It's tight, which makes for hilarious scenarios. At least for the viewers. Vanessa landed a role as Carmen in the 2005 episode 'The Coconut Kapow'. The only catch was that it turned out to be the last episode of *Quintuplets* ever made. Oh, well. You win some. You lose some. That's the up-and-down life of an actress.

When she got the role of Corrie on *The Suite Life*

of *Zack & Cody*, Vanessa definitely won one. *The Suite Life* isn't just a show. It's a phenomenon. Premiering on 18 March 2005, the Disney sitcom stars the adorable identical twins Dylan and Cole Sprouse as Zack and Cody – two kids whose lives get totally turned upside down when their mom (played by Kim Rhodes) snags a job at the Tipton Hotel. That's one of Boston's best hotels, and as part of their mother's deal, she and her twin sons get to live in one of the posh suites. So while Mom is slaving away at her job, the boys have the run of the place. They can swim in the pool, goof off in the game room, and annoy tourists in the lobby. There are also plenty of friends to make – including the rich and spoiled heiress London Tipton. The sweet and gorgeous Brenda Song plays London, and she couldn't be any more different in real life than her bratty character. But that's why they call it acting!

Zack and Cody make it their mission to pull all sorts of pranks, and it's up to nice-as-pie Maddie Fitzpatrick (the loveable superstar Ashley Tisdale) to stop them.

When Maddie isn't working at the hotel's candy counter, she's babysitting the twins. But she always has her eye on them. Her intelligence and quick reflexes keep the boys out of a lot of trouble. *The Suite Life* – created by Danny Kallis, from the TV show *Smart Guy* and *Family Matters* alum Jim Geoghan – has become a major hit among kids all over the country.

Vanessa was super lucky to get a chance to be on the show, even if it was only as a recurring character. She made her first appearance as Corrie – a perky schoolmate of Maddie and London – on the episode 'Forever Plaid', which aired in March 2006. On *The Suite Life*, her character is obsessed with snooty London and snubs Maddie at their school, Our Lady of Perpetual Sorrow. That's ironic, because in real life she's good friends with Ashley, who plays Maddie (but more on that later!). Anyway, there's no hard feelings since everyone on the show has such a great time while taping their episodes. 'It was so much fun because I'm really good friends with Brenda Song too, and Cole and Dylan are so adorable and

I knew them from before because I used to visit the set all the time. We just had a blast,' she told *Life Story*. 'We just hung out, worked, and had a blast. I'm enjoying every moment of all of this.'

Vanessa did so well during 'Forever Plaid' that the producers had her back for three more episodes: 'Not So Suite 16', 'Neither a Borrower Nor a Speller Bee', and 'Kept Man'. All the shows revolved around the Tipton gang, like in 'Not So Suite 16', where Maddie and London plan their sweet-sixteen parties for the exact same date. And they hang out with the exact same crowd! While Maddie attempts to be level-headed and convince London to change her plans, London won't hear of it, even though the party isn't on her actual birthday. London, who has buckets of cash to spend, lures more people to her fete with great food and favours, while Maddie ends up partying practically alone. Guess which party suck-up Corrie goes to?

The Suite Life might have been Vanessa's favourite show, but all the work she did on television also proved invaluable in moulding her career. The experience of working in such a fast-paced medium showed that Vanessa could handle the pressure. She could learn dialogue quickly, nail camera shots, get along with others and play lots of different types of characters. Vanessa had become a bona fide pro!

chapter 5

A Musical for the New Millennium

Ask anyone who works in the entertainment industry and they'll all tell you the same thing: mega-hits always seem so obvious in hindsight. A story about the adventures of a boy wizard at a private school in England? That can't miss! A reality television show in which undiscovered talents compete to become the country's next big star? What a sure thing! But as obvious as *Harry Potter* and *American Idol* seem to the world now, the fact is that someone had to think them up. And that's a lot easier said than done.

So it was with *High School Musical*. A couple of years back, a veteran television producer named Bill Borden was racking his brain trying to come up with a winning concept. After hours upon hours of brainstorming, a lightbulb finally went off in his mind. A major hit musical hadn't been made in years! That meant there was an entire generation of young fans who hadn't yet been whipped into a frenzy by a phenomenon like *Grease* or *West Side Story*.

Borden started to develop the idea right away. He knew that catchy showtunes would be a must, but he also wanted the musical to have a solid story line and a positive message. In the end, he decided that setting the story in a modern high school would allow him to touch on real themes. For inspiration, he looked to none other than William Shakespeare (arguably the greatest storyteller of all time). 'I wanted to create a Romeo-and-Juliet-type of story set in high school,' Borden told *Life Story* magazine. 'But rather than focus on feuding families, it would be the conflicts between different cliques that would work to keep the potential couple apart.' His working title was simple and direct: *High School Musical*.

The project seemed to have all the makings of a smash hit. But as difficult as it is coming up with winning concepts, selling other people on the idea can be even harder. At first, Borden couldn't get anyone to touch *High School Musical* (and you can bet they're all kicking themselves now!). After so many rejections, Borden was probably feeling pretty dejected when he sat down with the executives at the Disney Channel. But he shouldn't have been, because the genius behind his idea was about to be recognized. The top dogs at Disney ate it up!

Gary Marsh, president of entertainment for Disney Channel Worldwide, totally agreed with Borden that the lack of modern musicals represented a huge opportunity. Here's what he had to say to the *Orlando Sentinel*: 'Every decade has had an iconic musical: *West Side Story*, *Grease*, *Phantom of the Opera*, *Rent*. I'm hoping *High School Musical* becomes iconic for this decade. I believe twenty years from now kids will talk about the musical the way we talk about *Grease*.'

Disney pretty much gave Borden carte blanche with the project. Hoping to assemble the most talented team possible, his first step was hiring an up-and-coming screenwriter named Peter Barsocchini. The two immediately saw eye to eye on the themes the story should hit on. 'High school is such a polarized time,' Barsocchini explained to *Life Story* magazine. 'You've got the jocks, the brainiacs, the goths, the drama geeks – everyone has preconceptions about each other.' The goal with the script was to tackle these preconceptions head on. He continues: 'Disney wanted the film to focus on the real concerns of high school students in 2005 – which are really not that different from high school students in 1995. Even though it's a comedy, Disney did not want to condescend to kids.'

Borden and Barsocchini decided to set their story in a high school in Albuquerque, New Mexico. Unless you've been living under a rock for the past year, you're probably pretty familiar with the story, but here's a quick recap: a couple of teens named Troy Bolton and Gabriella Montez meet by chance at a karaoke club, where they end up singing a duet together. Mobile phone numbers are exchanged, but it looks like they're destined to be nothing more than two ships passing in the night. That is, until a week later when Gabriella shows up as the new girl at Troy's high school! It quickly becomes clear that, despite the chemistry they shared at the karaoke club, Troy and Gabriella come from very, very different worlds. He's the big man on campus, a star athlete who all the girls adore (cheerleaders in particular!). She's the shy, nerdy type, whose only real friends are team-mates from the school's academic decathlon squad. Still, despite their differences, Troy and Gabriella decide to try out for the musical together. This throws the school's social order into total upheaval, especially for Sharpay, the 'Queen Bee' who has been the star of the show forever. In the end, Troy and Gabriella have to decide if they're going to be ruled by pressure from their peers or by the passion in their hearts.

The story was exactly what Disney was hoping for – honest, sincere, and above all, positive in its outlook. 'Kids lives are awash in strife and stress, and this movie is optimistic, hopeful and celebratory,' Gary Marsh explained to the *Daily News of Los Angeles*. 'If being hopeful is corny, so be it. There's nothing wrong with being optimistic.'

With the story in place, the next step was finding the right director to handle the execution. Again, Borden tapped one of the best in the business, a man named Kenny Ortega. Best known for his work on films like *Dirty Dancing* and *Ferris Bueller's Day Off* and television shows like *Gilmore Girls*, Ortega had proven he could handle the challenges of a big production that had lots of moving parts. And like everyone involved in the project, he really believed that the timing was right for a modern musical. 'Young people don't get too many musicals,' Ortega told *Newsday*. 'It speaks of the time that they live in . . . We could go back and borrow from the classics, not reinventing the wheel, but do something for young people today that don't have the privilege of having music-driven stories.'

Ortega also agreed with the message behind *High School Musical*. 'I really like the idea of young people coming to know their own voice, regardless of outside pressure from peers, teachers, parents and society,'

Ortega told *The Courier-Mail*. 'There's too much bullying that goes on, and as a result kids back off from new ideas they have about themselves.'

By this time, the producers had made the decision to shoot the movie in Salt Lake City. Even though the story is set in New Mexico, the landscapes of the two locales look similar. Plus, the producers were able to find two high schools that would let them shoot the movie in their gym and classrooms (after school hours of course!). The choice of location was another fact that made Ortega the perfect director. He had choreographed the opening ceremonies of the 2002 Winter Olympics in Salt Lake City, so he was really plugged into the local community. It's no surprise that all but one of the extra background dancers came from Utah.

In addition, Ortega brought in several pop songwriting teams, each with a distinctive voice. This turned out to be a smart move, since the variety of styles adds to the terrific texture of the movie. The songs all sound different, ranging from catchy hip-hop to slow,

Vanessa Hudgens

Vanessa goes glam
at a *Vogue* event.

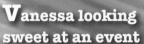

Vanessa looking
sweet at an event

The cast of *High School Musical*
gets dressed up!

Vanessa and
Miley Cyrus rockin'
the red carpet

Vanessa and her
co-star Corbin Bleu

Pretty as a picture

sentimental ballads. The songwriters were also required to incorporate actual lines from the script into their lyrics. 'We put a lot of pressure on the composers,' Ortega explains in *Life Story* magazine. 'It was important to me that the words were organic to the character and that they advanced the plot and gave you greater insight into the character. I'm really pleased they all accomplished that. The music really helps tell the story.'

With that, nearly all parts were in place. The script was tight, the director was ready, the music was strong, and the locations were all scouted and prepped. There was just one last thing the producers had to figure out: who were the actors going to be?

chapter 6
Most Likely to Succeed

When it comes to casting a movie, the conventional wisdom is this: go after the biggest stars possible so that you can draw in the most number of fans. That's why A-list celebrities like Lindsay Lohan and Hilary Duff get paid so much to appear in a picture. They have serious name recognition.

But the producers of *High School Musical* decided to take a different approach. This was partly out of necessity. After all, they only had a $4.2 million budget to play with. That sounds like a ton of money, until you realize that some movies cost hundreds of millions of dollars to make. On a production like that, four million dollars might be how much just one of the stars is getting paid!

Beyond the budget constraints, however, the

people in charge of casting *High School Musical* were looking for a very special breed of actor. The term that director Kenny Ortega used over and over was 'triple threats' – teenage performers who could act, dance and sing, not simply those who were famous.

In *Life Story* magazine, executive producer Bill Borden explained the game plan further: 'We brought people in and had them do a scene and read. Then we selected twenty-five or thirty who spent eight hours rehearsing in various combinations. It was really like a chorus-line audition. In the end we discovered six fresh faces. A movie like this allows kids that are talented to blossom.'

Vanessa Hudgens was among the hundreds of young performers who responded to the casting call. Although she was starting to get some traction as a television actor, she was hardly a sure thing going into the audition. Seeing the hordes of other hopefuls must have given her a lump in her throat. Whether it was nerves or not, Vanessa was definitely a little distracted during the auditions. So much so that she forgot what she was there for! She told *Entertainment Weekly* magazine, 'On the way to callbacks, I spaced and forgot I was trying out for a musical.'

One thing is for sure: it wasn't indifference that caused Vanessa to space out. Like any good actor, she was quickly learning how to determine which projects were duds and which had potential to turn into hits. On paper at least, *High School Musical* had the makings of a winner. 'Growing up doing musical theatre and seeing that the Disney Channel was going to be doing a musical, that automatically sparked my interest,' Vanessa told *Scholastic News Online*.

And yet, even with her interest going into the audition, there she was with absolutely nothing prepared. This looked like a recipe for disaster! But Vanessa didn't hit the panic button. Instead, she took a deep breath and belted out an a cappella version of Kelly Clarkson's 'Low'. The casting agents were suitably impressed (imagine if they had known that the performance was completely unrehearsed). They sent Vanessa through to the next round!

At this stage in the auditions, Vanessa must have sensed that she was super close to landing a part. But she wasn't there yet. Besides looking for teens who could sing and dance, the producers wanted to see tons of chemistry in front of the camera. That's why they kept trying out different combinations of actors. Eventually, Vanessa was matched with an adorable, brown-haired, blue-eyed guy named Zac Efron. 'There were hundreds of us auditioning,' Vanessa recalled in an interview with *The Calgary Sun*. 'Zac and I got paired up very early on. The big callback elimination audition lasted seven and a half hours. It was nerve-racking.' Seven and a half hours! That's a lot to ask even from the most seasoned of pros. But if the two beautiful brunettes were nervous, it didn't show. To the contrary, the way they interacted so naturally instantly caught the attention of everyone in the room. These kids didn't just have chemistry. They practically looked like soul mates!

Director Kenny Ortega was starting to sense that he had found his Troy and Gabriella. As he explained in *Life Story* magazine, 'For Gabriella we needed a beautiful, talented actress, but also someone who could really sing.' Vanessa fitted the bill on both counts, and she looked great next to Zac, who brought the exact cool-but-wholesome quality that defined the character of Troy.

Of course, nothing is just handed to you in Hollywood, and Vanessa and Zac were really put through the wringer during the very arduous audition process. 'We had to sing and dance and act,' Vanessa said in an interview with DallasNews.com. 'They sent us a song to learn, and we learned the dancing there. It wasn't like Gabriella and Troy, who stumble into the audition, stand by the piano, and sing and get a callback.' Eventually though, the producers made up their minds. Next to the role of Gabriella, they wrote the name Vanessa Hudgens!

chapter 7

Key Players

Vanessa was thrilled to land a lead part in the 'Disney musical', as the project was now being referred to in the industry. It looked like all the hard work she had put in doing local theatre and television commercials was starting to pay off. Maybe the most encouraging sign was the talent of her supporting cast. Let's meet the rest of the gang!

Zac Efron

Let's face it. Zac really doesn't need much introduction. Since *High School Musical*, his star has taken off faster than a rocket. Just like Vanessa, he's a native of California who got his start in community theatre (no wonder they get along so famously!). After doing a bunch of commercials, his first big break into serious television work came when he landed a recurring role in the popular television series *Summerland*. The show was about three siblings who are sent to live with their hip, slightly unconventional aunt in a West Coast beach community. Zac played the part of Cameron, the boy next door with a dark side. Even though *Summerland* was cancelled after just two seasons, it was a fantastic experience for Zac, allowing him to work with such established stars as teen rocker Jesse McCartney (who must have given Zac a tip or two about how to approach the musical!).

Even though Zac is one of the hottest guys out there, he's surprisingly modest and down to earth. In fact, he'd just as soon stay at home and work on one of his cars than go out partying until dawn. 'I don't want to be seen buying cigarettes and liquor,' Zac said to *Newsweek* magazine. 'It wouldn't be a smart move to be out doing promiscuous things.' That may be true, but there would be plenty of speculation about Zac's offscreen interest in some of his female castmates, including Vanessa. But that comes later in the story. For now, let's hear from the rest of the cast.

Ashley Tisdale

Though the hired cast included no already-established stars, Ashley Tisdale came pretty close. Born on 2 July 1985, in West Deal, New Jersey, Ashley was discovered at the tender age of three and has been moving steadily forward in her career ever since. She actually landed a part in the Broadway musical *Les Misérables* when she was just eight! But Disney fans will know her best from her starring role in *The Suite Life of Zack & Cody*, in which she plays the extremely likable candy-store clerk Maddie Fitzpatrick. Taking on the role of Sharpay, who might be better described as extremely unlikable (though someone you love to hate) was a major adjustment for Ashley. 'I don't wish I was like my character,' she told *Good Morning America*. 'I mean, only the part about my character that she loves to perform and she's got, you know, a great drive.' Making the switch from sitcom to movie was also an adjustment. 'With a sitcom, you have a live audience,' she explained in *Life Story* magazine. 'We go in, we rehearse, we're done by four or done by three and everything moves quickly. With a movie, they have to set up all the different shots. You block and then you film it, so it takes a lot of patience. But it's a very cool experience.' Her fans are enjoying Ashley's transition as well!

Lucas Grabeel

Lucas landed the part of Ryan Evans, Sharpay's twin brother and her co-conspirator in bringing down Gabriella and Troy. In real life, though, Lucas is a total sweetheart. He was born on 23 November 1984, in Springfield, Missouri. That happens to be the hometown of one of the biggest movie stars on the planet – Brad Pitt! Lucas will take that as a good sign. His mom actually contacted

Brad's mom to see if the established star had any wisdom for her own blue-eyed boy. 'And she actually called Brad and had him give me some advice before I left,' Lucas told *Good Morning America*. What did big Brad have to offer? 'His advice was to change my name,' Lucas continued. So far, Lucas is doing just fine with the name his parents gave him. Look for it in the credits of such hit television shows as *Veronica Mars*, *Boston Legal* and *'Til Death*, as well as the made-for-TV movies *In the Blink of an Eye*, *Halloweentown High* and *Return to Halloweentown*.

Corbin Bleu

The part of Chad, Troy's best friend from the basketball squad, was awarded to this super-cute actor from Brooklyn, New York. Corbin, who was born on 21 February 1989, is obviously a talented actor who knows how to move, but the thing that really sets him apart is that unmistakable shock of curly brown hair. 'I did have my hair shaved when I was eight,' Corbin admitted to

Good Morning America. 'But I enjoy my long hair. It's the epitome of me.' The ladies seem to agree, which is music to this self-proclaimed romantic's ears. 'I'm one of those guys that will put rose petals on the floor and that kind of thing,' Corbin told *Life Story* magazine. For the moment, though he is just trying to build up his career, which includes appearances on the television shows *Malcolm & Eddie* and *Hannah Montana*, as well as the films *Galaxy Quest* and *Catch That Kid*.

Monique Coleman

Born on 13 November 1980, Monique is one of the veteran actors in the cast. And it really shows from the expert way she handles the part of Taylor McKessie, the whip-smart (and occasionally calculating!) president of the academic decathlon team. In fact, Monique approaches every role with the same level of maturity and professionalism. 'I would like always to be known as an actress who is reliable and who always gives her best, and to be an actress who leaves her mark,' the South Carolina native told *Life Story* magazine. While Monique plays a maths whizz in the movie, in real life she actually prefers English and creative writing. 'But I can add. I can handle my finances!' she told *Newsweek* magazine. Obviously, this gal's talents run wide and deep! No wonder she's starred in everything from *Malcolm in the Middle* to *Gilmore Girls* to *Veronica Mars*.

Chris Warren Jr

Chris provides some of *High School Musical*'s most comical moments through his portrayal of the character Zeke Baylor. Remember? He's the one on the basketball team who, deep down inside, just wants to bake the perfect soufflé! Born on 15 January 1990 in California, Chris likes characters that are full of contradictions. Maybe because he is one himself in real life, being both an aspiring actor and the running back on his American football team. 'It's hard,' Chris admitted in an interview with *Life*

Story magazine. 'My parents have discussed my getting homeschooled to help juggle acting . . . but I really want to play high school football, because it keeps me normal and keeps me going.' Of course, Vanessa has been homeschooled since the age of eight, so Chris will have someone to relate to if he decides to go that route. His past acting credits include *The Bernie Mac Show*, *Any Day Now* and *Zoey 101*.

So there you have it: the cast of *High School Musical* (not counting the adults and almost three hundred extras, of course). Vanessa was pretty psyched to be part of such an amazing group of young actors. And everyone seemed to be really supportive as well, which is a good thing considering they were about to embark on one of the most gruelling work schedules ever imagined.

chapter 8
Action!

Making a movie is fun, right? It's easy being an actor, isn't it? Yeah, sure, and Simon Cowell from *The X Factor* is always super-friendly to the show's contestants! When Vanessa and the rest of the cast of *High School Musical* arrived on set, the sun was blazing hot and the director, Kenny Ortega, was even hotter. After all, the crew had fewer than twenty-five days to shoot the entire film, start to finish!

Fortunately, Vanessa was no stranger to long hours. 'The hardest part was having to work all day [because] it's tiring,' she told *Scholastic News Online*. 'But I loved every part of it, because I grew up in musical theatre, so I have been dancing [for a long time].' Still, nothing could have quite prepared her for the two weeks of 'boot camp' that

Ortega had in store for his actors. Given the awesome range of talents that would be on display in the movie, Ortega had no choice but to drive his performers.

'I've been dancing since I was two,' Corbin Bleu told *Newsweek* magazine, 'so for me that was second nature . . . We had basketball players who had never danced and dancers who had never played basketball. We were able to help each other. By the end of the training I was spinning a basketball on my fingertips.'

For eight hours a day or longer, Ortega had the actors singing, dancing and rehearsing – and that's before the first scene was shot. 'Yeah, the guys came back with shin splints, because they had to rehearse basketball after the dance rehearsal,' Vanessa told *Scholastic News Online*. 'It was long with the dance rehearsals and learning dances from morning to evening. We would be dancing our little butts away and Ashley and I were really trying to get into shape, so we would go to the gym at our hotel after the rehearsals.' Wow, going to the gym after you've danced all day. That's commitment.

With all the time they were spending together, Vanessa and Ashley were naturally becoming pretty tight. In no time, the two were practically best friends. Actually, the gals had met previously, but it was definitely the experience of *High School Musical* that made them as inseparable as they are today. Obviously, celebrity life is a little crazy at times. With the hectic pace of everyone's schedules, it's easy to fall out of touch fast. Plus, there's the added complication of jealousy between stars (sounds a little bit like real high school, huh?). But Vanessa and Ashley have found a way to keep their friendship intact, despite all those pressures.

The good, strong vibe that exists between Vanessa and Ashley definitely spread throughout the set. As hard as the crew worked during the day, they always found time to kick back together after shooting and at weekends. Sometimes they spent the entire afternoon swimming together in the pool of the Grand American Hotel, where they were housed for the duration of the shoot. Ashley and Vanessa liked to indulge in a little retail therapy. 'We stayed in a hotel, but we all stayed on the same floor relatively close to each other,' Vanessa told *Life Story* magazine. 'We just had a blast. We were all hanging out, watching movies, and Ashley and I would go shopping.'

On off days (not that there were many of those!), the entire gang would go sledding down the alpine slide in nearby Park City, Utah. Though when the girls got their way, it usually resulted in another hours-long shopping expedition. 'Fans are surprised to see the whole cast hanging together at the mall,' Ashley told *The Salt Lake Tribune*. 'Normally you wouldn't see the whole cast of *Ocean's Eleven* out at the mall.'

As much as they enjoyed the downtime, Vanessa and her castmates worked harder on *High School Musical* than ever before. For most of them, this was their first real taste of the demands of movie production. Fortunately, the director was one of the best leaders in the business. This man really knows how to inspire his actors. 'I thought the script was kind of generic,' Lucas Grabeel admitted to *Entertainment Weekly*. 'Once I met Kenny Ortega, I was like, "This may actually be something cool." ' Zac Efron agreed. 'It was like working with a big kid and his magic just rubbed off on all of us,' he told the *Sunday Express*. 'We all learned so much from [Ortega].' Zac admired Ortega for the way he stayed authentic to the material, even while rehearsing. 'It was Broadway style,' Zac told *Scholastic News Online*. 'We'd wake up at six in the morning and work until six at night. It was a very long day, but by the end I'd sustained so many injuries and was so sore but so much better than I was before. I learned more in those two weeks than I'd learned in the previous years.'

Even through the impossibly long and gruelling days, there was plenty of laughter on the set. Vanessa, who has always been able to giggle at herself, was often at the centre of the hilarity. Muffed lines were one of her specialties. As she recalled in *Scholastic News Online*, 'It's not embarrassing, but just so funny, because I look back at it and think, "Wow, Vanessa, you were so stupid."

There is a line in the movie where I see Troy for the first time in school and I say, "My mom's company transferred her here to Albuquerque." For some reason I could not say that line. I would get so tongue twisted and it's funny because I will watch it now and I have no idea why it was so hard for me back then.' Maybe it was all the dancing, working out and shopping?

In Vanessa's opinion, the fact that the set of *High School Musical* was such a raucous place to be directly influenced its success. The fun they had on set surely translated to the final product. 'The more relaxed we are, the more not-big-headed we are about it, the better we will be,' she told *The Salt Lake Tribune*. 'We all came into this just as normal people and had fun. If we do that, the fun we have shows on screen.'

As the days turned into weeks, it started to become apparent to everyone involved in *High School Musical*, from Vanessa right on down to the guys working the lights, that the project was unique. Of course, no one wanted to jinx it by making too many bold predictions, but a quiet confidence was definitely starting to fill the air. Monique Coleman explained it this way on CNN's *Showbiz Tonight*: 'There were moments, there were little glimmers shooting a couple of scenes that there's something special going here, specifically the finale. It was enough just to be able to do it.'

Vanessa, too, was starting to get her hopes up a little more each day. Maybe it was the way she and Zac seemed to be totally clicking in front of the camera. Or the amazing adrenaline that gripped the entire set during the filming of the movie's dramatic final scene. Whatever it was, the mood on the last day of shooting was definitely an optimistic one. Vanessa and the cast went their separate ways, confident that they had given their all, and hopeful that the fruits of their efforts would be recognized.

If Vanessa only knew just how widely she'd be recognized, and how crazy life was about to become, she might have opted for one last relaxing day by the poolside!

chapter 9
One for the Record Books

Cultural phenomena don't just happen every day. Once in a decade is more like it. In the late '70s and early '80s, *Star Wars* was maybe the biggest example. In the '90s, grunge music rose to the level of cultural phenomenon, thanks to bands like Nirvana and Pearl Jam. As for the first decade of the new millennium, there have definitely been a few whiffs of phenomena. *The X Factor* and *American Idol* have the makings. Websites like MySpace and Facebook have potential, too. But so far in the decade, one event seems to be leaps ahead of all other cultural phenomena. Its name, of course, is *High School Musical*.

Just take a look at some of the numbers: since *High School Musical* premiered in January 2006, it has been shown more than twelve times in America, and to over thirty-seven million viewers. That's more than the entire population of Canada! Then there's the soundtrack. Not only was it the number-one album of 2006 in America, having gone triple platinum, it's the first soundtrack to make it to the top of the Billboard chart. Ever!

But wait, there's more! The DVD of the movie is the fastest selling of all time – between May 2006 and August 2006, rabid fans bought more than 2.3 million copies. Then during awards season, *High School Musical* was nominated for six Emmys, and won the award for Outstanding Children's Programme. It also took home three Teen Choice Awards. Vanessa got in on that action, sharing the Best TV Chemistry award with Zac Efron. They do make a pretty cute couple!

Then there are all the spin-offs, from a book series featuring the private lives of the various characters to apparel, posters, stationery and other merchandise. Mattel has even introduced a *High School Musical* board game! On top of all that, adaptations of the movie are in the works for India and South America – they'll use cricket and football, respectively, instead of basketball.

There are also national US and UK tours of the stage adaptation and schools all over the world have staged their own productions of *High School Musical*. Imagine the chance to play the part of Gabriella in front of your entire school!

Geoff Mayfield, *Billboard* magazine's director of charts and senior analyst, told the *Chicago Sun Times* that *High School Musical* 'is the biggest surprise of the year . . . Album sales have grown every week it's been on the market – even weeks in which it wasn't number one, it still sold more than the prior week. No one saw it coming.'

There's no doubt about it: *High School Musical* is one of the biggest phenomena of the decade. But the question is: why? Vanessa still thinks it has to do with the message of the movie. As she explained to the *Chicago Sun Times*, 'The message of the film really is to break out of your clique. We're saying it's a good thing if you enjoy something like singing and dancing. Just do it. If your friends don't like it, then they're not your friends.'

Just as important, the movie's creators came up with

a cast of characters that kids really connect with. 'Wow, you can actually relate to the characters,' Patricia Kessanis, age fourteen, of Wayne, New Jersey, told *Newsweek* magazine. 'You have Sharpay, who's the snobby one you can't help but love to hate. You've got Gabriella, the quiet one, the brainiac, the smart one. You've got Troy, the basketball player who falls in love with the brainiac.' Vanessa herself seconded the idea that the made-up characters mirror real life when she told *The Calgary Sun*, 'We gave kids something new and different but something they could still relate to. *High School Musical* is the new cool thing.'

As with any cultural phenomenon, the popularity of *High School Musical* spread mainly by word of mouth. It's easy to imagine. In class, a couple of students are overheard talking about this great movie they watched last night. By third period, thirty kids know about it. By fifth period, one hundred kids. And by the end of the day, the entire school is buzzing with the news. This sort of thing happened all across the country.

Everyone was stunned (and thrilled) at how

quickly the *High School Musical* craze caught on. 'We had no idea it was going to be this big,' Vanessa said on *The Early Show*. 'But musicals haven't been done in such a long time for kids, it's something new . . . It's basically the same thing [as *Grease*]. The whole high school genre and everything. Without all the bad stuff. Gabriella doesn't wear the leather pants at the end of the story.' Well put!

Zac was as surprised as Vanessa, though it was the sales of the music that grabbed his attention. 'One thing led to another,' he told the *Cleveland Plain Dealer*. 'I went on to iTunes to buy music, and there we were. It's just a trip to know that we're up there with all these big people who I've been listening to growing up. We're travelling and going all over the world and doing tons of press for this movie.'

Practically overnight, Vanessa and her castmates had to get used to being worldwide celebrities. 'It's absolutely crazy,' Vanessa told *The Calgary Sun*. 'When fans see us in malls, they come up to us and sing the songs. Zac and I were in a lineup for a movie at a mall recently and a group of kids behind us not only began singing but did all the dance moves to one of the songs.' Zac, who has become the subject of countless teen magazine posters, admitted that he was flattered by all the newfound adoration, even strange singing in the mall. 'When I was younger I had a huge poster of Tyra Banks on the ceiling above my bunk bed,' he said in *The Calgary Sun*. 'I feel kind of honoured that girls would pin me up on their walls.'

Ashley Tisdale is also pretty psyched about all the attention, though she confesses that she doesn't totally understand it all. 'Apparently I'm the first female artist to have two songs debut on the top one hundred at the same time,' she told *The Calgary Sun*. 'It doesn't make sense. Like, I mean, that's just, like, crazy. It's crazy to think of all these singers and artists and stuff, and they're like, "You're the first female artist." And I'm like, "What? That's nuts." '

No matter where they go, cast members of *High*

School Musical are bound to get recognized – even in a place as full of stars as New York City. 'Monique and I were walking down the streets of New York,' Lucas Grabeel told *Life Story* magazine. 'This girl came up and she was like, "Oh my God. You guys are from *High School Musical*. I gave up *High School Musical* for Lent. I was watching it every day and it was getting in the way of all my stuff. So I had to give it up for forty days." ' Now that's devotion.

It was no different in the UK, when the cast arrived here to promote the movie. As Corbin Bleu told *Good Morning America*: 'I went to Madame Tussauds [in London] and had a little girl from Malaysia that actually came up to me and she recognized [me] . . . That was pretty cool.'

With international celebrity comes plenty of perks, as the cast was delighted to discover. When asked what the best part about being famous is, Vanessa didn't miss a beat: 'The free stuff,' she answered in the *Cleveland Plain Dealer*. 'Clothes. An iPod. I got a new TV from Disney, which was very generous. They gave the cast each a thirty-two-inch flat-screen TV.'

For Zac, the only thing better than celebrity swag (as the free handouts are known in the industry) is the exposure. 'The best perk is that going into the audition room, the casting director is at least somewhat familiar with your work, and that is always a big plus,' he explained.

There's no question that everyone who starred in *High School Musical* is getting more work because of it. 'It's been a stepping stone and it's a launching pad,' Vanessa told *Life Story* magazine. 'We're all on our way.' Zac, for example, landed a part in his first major motion picture. He plays the part of Link Larkin in the recent remake of *Hairspray*. It puts him in the company of some major A-list celebrities, including John Travolta, Queen Latifah and Amanda Bynes. You go, Zac!

Ashley Tisdale landed a role in the recent television series *Phineas and Ferb*, and she also recorded a music video for a remake of *The Little Mermaid*. Monique

Coleman landed maybe the most fun role: she was tapped to compete on the popular reality series *Dancing with the Stars* where celebrities are paired with professional dancers for a nationally televised dance competition. Actually, Vanessa was also approached by the show, but she told the *Cleveland Plain Dealer*: 'I had to confess I'd be eliminated instantly because I'm such a klutz. It just wouldn't be fair to the person they paired me with.' As for the rest of the cast, look for Lucas Grabeel in another Disney movie, *Halloweentown IV*, as well as in the music video he recorded for the DVD release of *The Fox and the Hound*. Corbin Bleu signed a recording contract with Hollywood Records and, like Lucas, he's also continuing his relationship with Disney, with a lead role in the movie *Jump In!*

Though the entire cast seemed to be going separate directions, they all stayed within the Disney family. Why? Because they'd all agreed to come back for *High School Musical 2*! Disney made the announcement after tons of clamouring from fans for more, more, more!

At first, the execs kept a pretty tight lid on the storyline, but the rumours started flying. It was pretty certain that the action was going to take place during summer vacation at the country club started by Sharpay's grandfather (who else!). 'It's still being written,' Vanessa had told the *Cleveland Plain Dealer*. 'We don't know much. I think it's been said that Sharpay will take an interest in Troy to get Troy away from me for the play that's going on over the summer. Something like that.'

While the stars of *High School Musical* didn't know what the script had in store for their characters, they definitely had their hopes. Vanessa, for one, wanted to see 'Troy and Gabriella finally get to kiss,' she told the *Cleveland Plain Dealer*. 'From the mail I get, that's definitely what our fans want.' In general, she'd like to see Gabriella take some more chances and inspire others to do the same. 'Maybe my character will break out of her shell a little more,' she speculated on *Good Morning America*. 'I think that if Gabriella kind of steps out of that, it will show the girls they can, too.'

Always a bit of a ladies' man, Zac had other ideas: '[I hope] they'll write a guest spot for Paula Abdul as a dance instructor. Maybe she could turn us into actual dancers.' As for the character of Sharpay, fans could expect more of the same backstabbing and manipulation (all done with a smile, of course!). 'I don't think [she'll mellow],' Ashley said on *Good Morning America*. 'I think she's going back for revenge.'

Whatever plot twists were in store, one thing was guaranteed: the sequel was going to carry the *High School Musical* phenomenon solidly into 2007. But for Vanessa, the movie was just one of many huge events to happen that year.

chapter 10
Tuning In

The *High School Musical* soundtrack broke about every record around, and at the centre of its success was Vanessa's duet with Zac, 'Breaking Free'. Fans, critics and music industry folks freaked out over this little album that exploded on the charts. So it was only a matter of time before record producers started banging down Vanessa's door to get her to record her own album. They didn't wait long. Practically overnight, she had a lot of offers to keep singing.

But Vanessa was torn about moving from the small screen to the recording studio. Along with the rest of the *High School Musical* gang, she had experienced fame and fortune beyond her wildest dreams through TV. Why not just concentrate on that medium and continue to stoke a red-hot acting career? 'I'm actually still in a state of shock over the film because of all the credit we've been given for it, and just how much it's blown up,' she told Life Story at the time of HSM's opening. 'It's just insane. Now I'm going to try and go off and do my own solo album, but I'm like, "I'm already number one. Where do I go from here?"' Good question.

What if she recorded an album and it was a big flop? Vanessa had no assurances that her music would take off like her acting. But she never shied away from a challenge. And with the best music producers in the business dying to work with her, how could she say no? 'Acting is my first priority, but I have the opportunity now to work on my own solo album, so I'm gong to pursue that,' she told the Cleveland Plain Dealer. 'Acting always will be my number one.'

Okay, if acting was number one, then music would become a close second for Vanessa. She didn't want to put out a lame-o, boring album, so she had a lot of work ahead of her in order to create sounds she and her friends would think were cool. Vanessa's big goal for her album was to break out of the ordinary genres. She didn't want to make a purely pop record, or something completely R&B. She loves Latin music but didn't want that to be the only influence either. Vanessa dreamed of producing something unique, something 'kinda soulful and kinda rock,' she told the *San Antonio Express-News*. That sounds just like her, 'very eclectic'.

Perplexed over what direction to take her first solo album, Vanessa was kind of all over the place. 'I'm trying to do something different,' she told *Life Story*. 'I'm trying to do pop rock, but with a dance flair. Something fun. Or pop rock with a jazzy big band flair, because my grandparents are both big band musicians, so I would love to contribute something to that. I just love jazz.' That's a lot to get into one album!

It's not surprising that she hoped for an eclectic mix, considering the wide range of music she enjoys. Her desire to create music out of a lot of different styles is reflected in her extensive CD collection. Vanessa loves the soulful ladies who can belt out a serious tune such as Alicia Keys and Celine Dion. And ever since she bought the soundtrack to *Smallville*, she's been really into KT Tunstall. But Vanessa buys a ton of music online – some of her other faves include Zero 7, Yeah Yeah Yeahs, Wu-Tang Clan, The Blood, Sublime and The Postal Service. The Wu-Tang Clan and Celine Dion? Now that's an eclectic mix. Vanessa's not exactly proud of every album in her CD collection. While hanging out with a friend, she even picked up the Paris Hilton CD. 'We were kinda bored,' she said, making an excuse to JustJared.com.

On 12 June 2006, Hollywood Records made it official. The company announced an exclusive recording deal with Vanessa. She was going to be a real-live recording artist. The news was super exciting. Vanessa had a whole new world open to her, new challenges, new songs to write, and of course new outfits to pick. But she had a lot of pressure and work ahead of her to make the quick turnaround the record company planned. When they announced the deal, they also said the CD was down for release on 26 September. Yikes!

Poor Vanessa had only about three months to put her first album together! Buena Vista Music Group Chairman Bob Cavallo wasn't worried. 'We are delighted to have Vanessa at Hollywood,' he said in the announcement. 'Not only is she talented, she is tireless in her work ethic and has a vision for her career. People will be very impressed when they hear her voice and see her perform.'

It was the beginning of a process Vanessa called 'gruelling'. First she combed musical styles and songs to see what she liked and what she didn't. Then she visited a bunch of recording studios to get the hang of it and find a producer who would be a good fit for her singing style. 'That was really tiring,' she told JustJared.com. One producer told her to stop pronouncing her words so clearly when she sang (a habit held over from her musical theatre days). Then almost immediately after, another told her to pronounce her words more clearly. What's a girl to do? As she told JustJared.com, she thought to herself, 'I'm never going to get this right . . . I put tears and laughter into it. But it's like a journey.'

This taxing journey had a happy ending. Finally, after an exhaustive search, Vanessa found music producer Antonina Armato. They ended up having an awesome time in the studio together. Antonina loved to joke around with Vanessa and even gave her a new nickname, Baby V, which wound up in the album's lyrics.

Now, an album can completely rock, but if the first single isn't catchy, the whole project can be doomed instantly. Vanessa's single had to be the highlight, or calling card, for the rest of the CD. She had to entice listeners with millions of choices to listen to *her*. 'Come Back to Me' did the trick. Exploding with energy, danceable but also singable, this song about missing a guy had an upbeat feeling despite its theme. Not taking any chances, Vanessa used the best when sampling for her single. The underlying sample of her song is 'Baby Come Back' by the late 1970s group Player. It was actually their biggest single, hitting number one on the Billboard Hot 100 in 1978. So Vanessa had a Billboard-proven hit propping her up. But that was ancient history.

To bring her single back to present day, she included rapper T.I., who announces Baby V in the beginning of the song and performs throughout. That definitely gave sweet Vanessa's sound some edge. Leader of the rap group P$C (Pimp Squad Click), T.I. put out his first album *I'm Serious* in 2001. But it was his second album, *Trap Muzik*, that brought serious success. Unfortunately, that success was also followed by serious trouble. While T.I. (his real name is Clifford Joseph Harris Jr) was on tour, he violated his probation over a 2003 drug charge. T.I. eventually turned himself in and received three years in prison.

Can you believe Vanessa recorded a song and appeared in her video with an ex-con? The tiny star can obviously hang with seriously tough guys. That may be true, but T.I. turned out to be a good guy as well. In the aftermath of Hurricane Katrina, he has done a lot to raise money for the victims, including personally donating fifty thousand dollars toward the relief effort. That's not all. T.I. has worked with troubled youths and offered scholarships for kids from single-parent families. The rapper has clearly learned his lesson, changed his ways and is repaying his debt to society.

Vanessa had a total blast making her video, which she shot in only a few days. 'It was such a great two days,' she told Aol.com. 'My little toy poodle even got a little part!' It pays to have connections. Directed by Chris Applebaum, the 'Come Back to Me' video shows a completely different side to Vanessa than what came through with her *HSM* character, Gabriella. There is nothing nerdy about Vanessa as she dons super-cute outfits, super-tall heels and super-sexy make-up, all while dancing by herself. She's got the wind blowing her gorgeous hair and everything. Was it hard for her to dance around solo for the entire song? 'It is because all eyes are on you!' she told JustJared.com. 'It's not like where you're with an entire group of people.' While filming *HSM*, a typical dance scene could have dozens of kids. Now it was simply the Vanessa show. But in the end, she found the pressure freeing. 'I could just let loose because I didn't have to blend in with everybody. I could just do whatever I wanted,' she told JustJared.com.

Luckily, a lot of her old pals were on the set, including Gary Marsh, the entertainment president for Disney Channel Worldwide. Was he checking up on young Vanessa to make sure her outfits and dance moves didn't get too racy for Disney's wholesome image? While Gary says he and the rest of the people running Disney would never do anything to break the trust that parents have placed in their channel, they don't lord their power over their stars. 'They're all independent . . . There is no manifesto,' he told *The Arizona Republic*. 'What we can do is counsel them.'

Whatever advice he had for Vanessa seems to have worked, since her music career quickly gained momentum. On 15 August, Hollywood Records released a compilation CD called *(Lip Smackers Presents) Girl Next*, featuring today's biggest female recording artists from Hilary Duff to Aly & AJ to Kelly Clarkson. And guess who was included? That's right, Vanessa snagged track number six for her song 'When There Was Me and You'. It was a serious honour to have the spot right after Everlife's 'Real Wild Child'.

On August 19, 'Come Back to Me' first hit the airwaves on Radio Disney, and about a week later it was released to all radio stations. Finally Vanessa's fans could hear her sing: 'Baby come back to me / I should've never set you free / Love maybe / Come back.' It's kind of hard to imagine Vanessa grovelling for some guy to come back to her, but it was still fun dance music.

The first music video from the album, for the song 'Come Back to Me', premiered on the Disney Channel on 25 August 2006. Disney prized Vanessa so much that the channel gave her video premiere a top spot, right after *The Cheetah Girls 2* movie, as a way of capping off its So Hot Summer programme.

Only a month later, the moment of truth arrived. On 26 September 2006, Vanessa released her debut album entitled *V*, in honour of herself. Well, sort of (hey, she put all that work into it, she deserved a little credit).

Vanessa explains the title's meaning: 'Of course it stands for Vanessa, but it also stands for Variety because my album is kind of a mix tape,' she told JustJared.com. 'It's just a wide mix of things. I recorded it pretty quick and I'm really happy with what I did.' She achieved her original goal of making an album with a variety of songs.

As soon as her album dropped, Vanessa was off and running again. She had appearances on *Good Morning America*, *TRL*, *Live with Regis and Kelly* and loads of other places. But if you think Vanessa got a big head from being a world-famous actress and pop star, think again. To kick off her debut album, she didn't host some fancy, elite red-carpet party. No, she celebrated with a barbecue!

Vanessa remained humble because she's smart and knows that no matter how great you are as a singer, it's really hard to make a dent in the music business. Because of all the albums coming out, it's easy for any particular record to get lost in the shuffle. The odds were really stacked against Vanessa getting her music to the people. But then she got a super lucky break.

chapter 11
Getting in on the Girl Power

As big a hit as *High School Musical* has been, there's one other teen-targeted cultural phenomenon that has rivalled its success in America: The Cheetah Girls. It's not surprising, considering the two ventures are similar in so many ways. First of all, they're both products of Disney (whose executives must be doing cartwheels down their office hallways!). Second, they both contain tons of catchy songs and cool dance numbers. Third, they both send out a totally positive message that kids can really relate to. And last but not least, they both include Vanessa!

Actually, The Cheetah Girls was already pretty well established when Vanessa jumped on board. Its story goes all the way back to 1999, when an author named Deborah Gregory published a book about four aspiring singers in New York City who were desperate to land their first record deal. She entitled it *The Cheetah Girls*.

Something about the story struck a chord with readers. Its main characters are an ethnically diverse group of gals with distinctive characteristics. There's Galleria, the headstrong leader of the band. Chanel is the shy, sensitive one whose mom is involved with a Spanish aristocrat. Then there's the super sassy and fashionable Aqua. Lastly is Dorinda, the foster child with a heart of gold.

Despite their differences, there is one thing that brings these girls together. Well, two things actually: they can sing, and they can dance. The problem with the book was that you couldn't hear the music or see the moves. Disney sensed an opportunity. In 2003, the company brought the characters to life with its release of *The Cheetah Girls* movie. They'd found the perfect four actors: Raven-Symone, who started on *The Cosby Show*, would play Galleria. Adrienne Bailon, from the urban hip-hop band 3LW, landed the role of Chanel. Kiely Williams, also a member of 3LW, got the part of Aqua. And Sabrina Bryan, who had appeared in several episodes of the soap opera *The Bold and the Beautiful*, would play Dorinda.

As expected, the movie was a big hit with viewers. Sales of the DVD would eventually top two million. But that was just the beginning. On the strength of the film, Disney decided to follow up the soundtrack with a holiday album called *Cheetah-licous Christmas*. First, The Cheetah Girls went from the pages of a book to the television screen. Now they were evolving into a real-life pop band!

As fiction turned into reality, the message of The Cheetah Girls really started to come into focus. The group's ethos came down to two words: Girl Power. In this sense, The American Cheetah Girls seemed to be picking up where the British Spice Girls left off!

The Cheetah Girls took that positive message of empowerment even further. 'We're always concerned about that kind of thing,' Adrienne Bailon told *The Arizona Republic*. 'I think that's what the whole meaning of The Cheetah Girls is, to be positive for those girls out there.'

Adrienne wanted to tear down false myths about girls and women through her music and movies. 'Girls always get the reputation of being catty,' she told the *Biloxi Sun Herald*. 'But I think what The Cheetah Girls stand for is supporting one another and sticking together.'

Disney knew it had a good thing in The Cheetah Girls, so the company wasted no time planning a sequel. They also sent the band on tour where they would generate even more ferocious Cheetah buzz. Both moves proved to be wise and profitable.

First, the movie: in the sequel's clever plot twist, Chanel is carted off to Barcelona, Spain, where her mother has gone to be with her European boyfriend. The other Cheetahs, showing true support and solidarity, follow Chanel to this foreign land, where they end up competing in a singing competition. Disney brought in Kenny Ortega, who of course directed *High School Musical*, to head up the production. Between Ortega's expertise and the majestic filming location, the excitement on set was palpable. 'We were really excited to be together again and to do something for our fans,' Kiely told the *Biloxi Sun Herald*. 'But being on the streets of Barcelona and seeing all those architectural marvels was unforgettable.'

All those good, strong vibes clearly found their way on to the screen. In fact, as popular as the original Cheetah Girls proved, the sequel was one for the record books. Its premiere in August 2006 drew 7.8 million Disney viewers. Believe it or not, that's actually more than *High School Musical*!

The Cheetah Girls tour, meanwhile, experienced even grander success. Kicked off in September 2006, it included over forty cities across America. At each stop, The Cheetah Girls were greeted by scores of screaming fans, most of them decked out in Cheetah-print attire. The Cheetah Girls always responded with a super-charged, high-energy concert. Often, the show would last more than three hours. Clearly, these cats know how to put on a show!

Part of the success of The Cheetah Girls is the fact that they draw on such different musical influences. Kiely is into a lot of old-school stuff. 'I really like the Steve Miller Band. I like a lot of classic rock,' she told *Scholastic News Online*. For Sabrina, it's 'Gwen Stefani, and I really like Madonna, what she's done with her career, and her style.' Then there's Adrienne, who said: 'I love girl groups, En Vogue, SWV, TLC.'

Because of their wide-ranging influences, The Cheetah Girls are a very flexible group. In the course of a single set, their sound can go from dance to hip-hop to Latin. They can also take on new members really easily. That's why no one panicked when Raven-Symone, the leader of the band, announced that she wouldn't be able to make the tour. Instead, they looked around for guest performers who shared their eclectic tastes. Vanessa was a perfect fit. After all, the playlists on her iPod range from Celine Dion to the Yeah Yeah Yeahs.

The Cheetah Girls must have been growling with excitement when Vanessa agreed to join the tour (also signing on for a stint was Miley Cyrus, star of the Disney Channel's *Hannah Montana*). 'We are so excited!' Sabrina gushed in the *Biloxi Sun Herald*. 'We're going to sing a remake of "Girls Just Wanna Have Fun" with Miley and Vanessa,' she said, referring to the hit '80s tune by Cyndi Lauper. This was a Cheetah Girls first. 'We've never had anyone on stage with us before, so it's going to be exciting,' Sabrina said. 'We're hoping to do another movie and we want to keep The Cheetah Girls alive as long as we possibly can.'

The timing couldn't have been more perfect for Vanessa. Her first album debuted at the end of September, and she was down to join The Cheetah Girls in the middle of October. This was just the boost she needed for her album to get some serious recognition. But it was a gruelling schedule, with concerts held just about every day. One week, the band was in Washington, DC. The next, they were up in Providence, Rhode Island. Then it was over to Saint Paul, Minnesota. 'It's been so crazy,' Sabrina told *The Daily News of Los Angeles*. 'Our schedule is so hectic that I had to get up at three o'clock in the morning just to get my roots done.'

Fortunately, Vanessa was used to hard work and up to the challenges of life on tour. When she wasn't up onstage with The Cheetah Girls, she'd find ways to recharge. 'I'm bringing my computer,' she told JustJared. com. 'It keeps me preoccupied very well.' Maybe Vanessa *is* just a little bit geeky like Gabriella.

It's not hard to picture Vanessa tapping away on her computer each night (maybe even still decked out in her Cheetah prints!). No doubt she was inspired by the experience and was cranking out lyrics for her next solo album. She probably also sent frequent e-mails to her friends and family back home, maybe filling Ashley in on the latest happenings or giving her kid sister, Stella, more words of encouragement. Some nights, Vanessa must have also found time to record a few thoughts in her private journal. Who knows what she wrote exactly, but it was definitely the musings of a star whose future was getting brighter with every passing day.

chapter 12

Friendly Faces

Movies, music, touring, television: with all this going on, how does Vanessa keep sane? Like anybody else – with a little help from a few good friends. Sure, Vanessa definitely doesn't have a normal life with school, chores, and a job during the weekend. But that doesn't mean she can't have friends like a normal person.

Vanessa has talked openly about how it was hard for her to find close companions while growing up since she didn't attend regular school and moved around a lot. But Vanessa is way too sweet to be solo for long. Nowadays she has a close-knit group from working in Hollywood, where she found stars just like herself. 'All my friends are pretty much older than me or in the business, so we all understand each other,' Vanessa told *Scholastic*

News Online. 'I haven't been to real school since I was in seventh grade, so I don't know very many people out of the business.'

Vanessa is nothing if not a loyal friend. She even gave best bud, actress Alexa Nikolas, a part in her video for 'Come Back to Me'. Alexa and Vanessa know each other from around the Disney way. A Chicago native born in 1992, Alexa is a big star on the channel. She's been on *The Suite Life of Zack & Cody*. Alexa has also been featured on Nickelodeon's *Zoey 101*. A funny fact is that she has the same birthday as her *Zoey* co-star Jamie Lynn Spears, and they both have the same breed of dog for a pet. Putting Alexa in her video was partly selfish of Vanessa. How fun is it to have your good friend around while you wear the hottest fashions, dance around and lip-synch to your own music video? Plus, they complement each other really well. With her dark hair and light skin, Alexa makes a pretty counterpart to Vanessa's dark and exotic looks.

When Vanessa is hanging out with her friends, she

loves to do ordinary kid stuff. 'We dress up crazy and take tons of pics!' she told Teen magazine. Of course she and her famous friends have much better clothes than the average kid to dress up in. And like any normal kid, Vanessa is positively tied to her mobile phone and computer. But because she's so busy working and travelling all the time, her gadgets keep her close to her friends. In fact, when she wakes up, the first thing she does is grab her phone and check for any text messages or calls that she missed.

Of course, everyone knows that Vanessa is tight with the entire High School Musical gang. Even though they get along great, when the TV movie first aired, the cast had to do so much publicity that it was almost too much together time. 'Every time I've been out, it's been with these guys,' Vanessa told TeenMusic.com at the time. 'I really don't have time to meet anyone.' Now Vanessa can only look back on those times with fondness.

The HSM cast has scattered across the country, each with an equally busy schedule. Disney often brings them together, which helps. They all hooked up for the

Disney Channel Games in April 2006. Reunited with Corbin Bleu and Monique Coleman, Vanessa played on the Blue Team, which took first place with a little assistance from other Disney stars like *The Suite Life*'s Brenda Song and Cole Sprouse, and *Hannah Montana*'s Jason Earles.

Sure, Vanessa cares about everyone on *HSM*, but her very best pal is Ashley Tisdale! 'My family are the ones who will always be there for me, whereas some friends come and they go,' she told *Life Story* magazine. 'But now and then you find a really loyal friend.' That definitely describes Ashley. Vanessa has other adjectives to describe her BF including 'sweet', 'funny', and 'crazy', as she said in *Life Story*. Ashley has equally nice things to say, describing Vanessa in an interview with TV.com as 'thoughtful, trustworthy, kind, and considerate'.

The two have a history that goes beyond *High School Musical*. Ashley and Vanessa actually met two years before the hit Disney musical on a commercial for Sears, where they both had to dance. Although their friendship didn't deepen until later, they liked each other immediately. So when they both landed on the same TV project, they were ecstatic. 'The first time we saw each other, after we knew we had got *High School Musical*, was in the recording studio,' Vanessa told *Life Story*. 'We just ran to each other, screamed, and jumped up and down like a pair of little girls. We were just so excited.'

The fun didn't end there. The two girls had a ball working together. They laughed like crazy, even when they messed up on set. During filming 'Stick to the Status Quo', one of the last musical numbers, Ashley was walking down a flight of stairs. The plan was for her to flip her hair in a snotty way and walk over to Vanessa. Although she was wearing flats, Ashley experienced a major wardrobe malfunction. Her shoes weren't on right. 'I fell out of my shoes and tripped. I think that was one of the funniest things, and Vanessa is just standing there and laughing,' Ashley told *Life Story*. 'I was really hysterical.' Apparently, Vanessa's not the only one who can laugh at herself.

Like Vanessa, most of Ashley's friends are actors – although she keeps a group of good buds back in New

Jersey, where she was born. 'But a lot of my friends are in the business,' she told *Life Story*. 'It is easier to relate to them.' What about all the competition that actors must feel when they hang out together? They pretty much go for the same parts in the same shows. How can they go out to dinner or the movies after auditions? 'I have never been competitive,' Ashley said in *Life Story*. That was a lesson from her mom. 'That's a good thing because in this business it can get into competition and people can be really mean.' But not everybody's like that. So when Ashley finds other nice folks in show business, like Vanessa, she holds on to them. 'It can be really nice to know that they know me and they understand what actors go through, because they are actors themselves.'

Although Ashley and Vanessa are celebrity BFFs, their friendship is based on what many friendships are: honesty. '[Ashley's] very loyal to me. If we have a problem with each other, we tell each other,' Vanessa told *Life Story*. 'We won't let it sit in the back of our minds; we'll actually tell each other that there's something bothering us so our relationship doesn't get hurt.' That's a change from the typical image all over magazines of celebrities backstabbing each other.

When Ashley and Vanessa hang out, they make quite a scene together. They aren't just pretty, stylish, good at dancing and fun – they're famous! *High School Musical* and *The Suite Life* fans go insane when they catch the pair out in public. 'When I go out with Ashley, they just kind of scream at us,' Vanessa told *Scholastic News Online*. Despite the craziness and drama, Ashley and Vanessa don't hide behind velvet ropes in VIP sections, hanging out only with other celebrities. They like to go to the movies and the mall like anybody else. Vanessa keeps herself open to all kinds of people. 'When I was in "real" school, I kind of just learned that cliques cause drama,' she told TeenMusic.com. 'You're better off to mingle with everybody. Be in a good crowd with everybody to avoid the drama. I hate drama. I really do.' That's a pretty important lesson to learn, especially by seventh grade!

chapter 13

What About Love?

When you're cute and perky, with plenty of talents and smarts to go along with it, people are bound to take notice. Sooner or later, they start to wonder: is she seeing anyone? Vanessa definitely gets her share of attention. And as one of the hottest stars to break on to the scene, there's no shortage of speculation about her love life.

The rumour mill was going especially hard on the set of *High School Musical*. And why wouldn't it? The movie pulled together a bunch of the brightest and most beautiful young actors in the business – much to the delight of Zac! 'That was one of the benefits of being in the movie,' he told TeenMusic.com. 'Lots of pretty girls.'

Zac definitely took notice of Vanessa right away. They were paired up early on in the audition process, so they had a bond going before the other cast members were even hired. When they were tapped for the lead roles of Troy and Gabriella, the relationship only grew more intense. By that point, the rumours were really starting to fly. When *Entertainment Weekly* asked Zac what his fans are most curious about, he replied: 'They usually want to know if I'm dating anyone in the cast.' But is it any wonder? After all, Hollywood is teeming with stories of onscreen connections turning into real-life love affairs, from Humphrey Bogart and Lauren Bacall all the way up to Brad Pitt and Angelina Jolie.

Vanessa and Zac definitely had that kind of presence. Don't forget, they would eventually take home the Teen Choice Award for TV Chemistry. Plus, Zac really seemed to be Vanessa's type. Just listen to her description of Mr Right on Teenmag.com: 'I like surfer guys and guys who are taller than me, which is not hard because I'm only 5´ 3˝. I usually like darker hair and lighter eyes so there's a contrast and having a nice body helps.' Does that sound like someone familiar? Vanessa has a few more demands, including 'a fun personality and someone who isn't afraid to be stupid and act like a kid and make me laugh'.

Zac definitely fits the bill of what Vanessa's looking for in a guy. So, did they end up becoming more than just co-stars? During the filming of *High School Musical*, it appears they kept their affections in check! 'No, I don't think there were necessarily any on-set romances,' Zac recalled on TeenMusic.com. 'But we immediately all became fast friends. We got a good group, which is very rare. There wasn't a bad seed among any of the kids.'

Still, even if there wasn't any hanky-panky on the set, Zac and Vanessa did share their first kiss, however inadvertently. 'We did get to kiss – by accident!' Zac admitted to the *Sunday Express*. 'In the story, Chad [Troy's best friend, played by Corbin Bleu] was supposed to come between us before we kissed, but he was too late, so they just cut the film.' So Zac did sneak in a quick peck on the lips.

So was there more smooching in store for Vanessa and Zac? Well, the audience got its way – Troy and Gabriella shared their first onscreen kiss in *HSM 2*. 'I know the fans want Troy and Gabriella to finally kiss,' Vanessa told TeenMusic.com. And as their *HSM* romance blossomed on screen so did their real-life relationship because it's no secret that they're now dating! On CBS's *The Early Show*, Vanessa admitted, 'I try to keep it under wraps just because I'm a very private person and I like to keep my personal life to myself.' So don't expect Vanessa to spill the beans any time soon!

chapter 14

A Day in the Life

Sure, Vanessa is so gorgeous that she landed a swimsuit television commercial for Old Navy. And she can sing so well that she has her own album. *And* she's had a hit TV movie that will be shown all over the world. So she's a true superstar. But that doesn't mean Vanessa isn't like any ordinary girl who enjoys ordinary things such as friends, family and theme parks. Because she does.

First off, Vanessa has to blow off steam like any typical kid. But one way you won't find her doing that is karaoke. Although it changed her character Gabriella's life, Vanessa has only tried it once with friends. They went out to a karaoke club and chose 'Say My Name' as their song. But they quickly discovered they didn't know any of the words. 'We just blew it,' she told *Teen* magazine. That was the last time for Vanessa on the karaoke machine.

To unwind, she would rather crack open a good book, like *Memoirs of a Geisha* by Arthur Golden, which she recently read. But when Vanessa really needs to escape the pressure of a top celebrity's busy life, there's no better way than hitting a horror movie. 'I get so scared at scary movies,' she told JustJared.com. 'My mind totally takes me on a ride.' Even though she likes them, Vanessa has a really low fright tolerance. She jumps out of her skin when she sees the trailer for a horror flick alone.

In general, Vanessa has no problem kicking back in front of the telly. She loves really scary movies, but Vanessa also loves totally tasteless humour. She finds TV shows like *Family Guy* and *South Park* hilarious. She also enjoys zoning out to teen dramas like *Degrassi*. But when a gaggle of friends comes over to watch something, Vanessa always reaches for the same DVD to pop into the player. She forces everyone to watch *Moulin Rouge*, a dreamy musical starring the gorgeous Nicole Kidman and the sexy Ewan McGregor. 'I'm a hopeless romantic,' she told *Teen* magazine.

When she's watching TV with her family, the choice is entirely different. Vanessa forgoes the sensual musical for something a little more youthful – but still romantic! 'If we have nothing to do we watch *The Tenth Kingdom*,' she told *Teen* magazine. 'It's a six-hour movie: two worlds connected by a secret door to a fairy-tale land where Snow White and Cinderella live. It's so cute.' That's a lot of TV time with the folks!

One time when it's particularly hard for Vanessa to relax is at night. No matter how much she has done that day, Vanessa becomes totally awake when the sun sets. 'At night, that's when my energy goes up again,' she told JustJared.com. 'I usually just wear off my energy . . . I get my second wind at night. I kind of like go crazy and I'm really energetic and I jump all over the place and I just crash.'

Maybe her energy bursts are actually sugar highs in disguise. Vanessa is a total chocolate junkie. She can't get enough of the rich, dark stuff. 'You give me any kind of chocolate, I will eat it, believe me! I'm addicted,' she says on her website, vanessaannehudgens.net. 'Ever since I was little, I've always loved chocolate. I even have it by my bedside.' And she wonders why she can't relax at night?

With all the TV and chocolate, it's unbelievable that Vanessa is as petite as she is. Well, she doesn't just eat chocolate and lie around like a couch potato all day. She exercises at the gym and runs around the block to get her heart rate up. Chasing her dog Shadow around burns a lot of calories as well. Not to mention what great exercise she gets dancing around in her own videos and practising for *High School Musical 2* and *3*. Vanessa doesn't need to go to the gym when she's got a choreographer working her to the bone!

The tiny star also watches what she eats. A superstar can't live on junk food alone. Vanessa doesn't think twice about making a meal of sushi, which is very low in fat. But you won't see her get anywhere near a carrot. That's where the health train stops. 'They make me gag,' she told *Teen* magazine. As to her cooking skills, those are pretty limited. Vanessa's speciality is barbecued steak. And that's about it. 'I leave the cooking to my mom,' she told *Teen* magazine. Luckily her mother enjoys taking care of her daughters.

You already know that Vanessa and her family are super close. In fact, she calls her family her most 'prized possession'. Her parents are really protective of their oldest daughter, but they also trust her because of the good relationship they have forged over the years. Vanessa doesn't even have a curfew! But her mom does have to know where she is when she's out. Sounds fair.

Vanessa's family understands her and the pressure she feels every day. They love her for who she is, not because she's pretty or because she's a famous star. They accept her no matter how goofy she acts. Vanessa loves them back for it: so much so, she even dreams about them. 'It was so random and it felt so real. My sister was marrying a cupcake,' she confided in *Teen* magazine about a vivid dream. 'And then a cupcake shot up in the air and made cupcake babies and there were a whole bunch of them. My dad was like, "This is a suitable husband for you." So I married a cupcake too!' Um, okay? At least her dad is a supportive guy, even in her dreams.

Cupcakes aren't the only things Vanessa dreams about. She also dreams, daydreams anyway, about owning a Porsche. But she needs a little more practise time behind the wheel before she's ready for the powerful sports car. She told *Teen* magazine that it's surprising 'how hard it is to park the car along the kerb'. Yikes! No matter how cool she is, you might want to think twice before getting a ride with Vanessa.

Fashion is one area where Vanessa doesn't need any tutoring. She has a great, effortless style that's been praised by many reporters and producers who have crossed her path. Vanessa looks sophisticated and cool but totally age appropriate. She's not one of those teen stars trying to dress like she's forty years old.

Maybe that's because Vanessa doesn't rely on a

fashion stylist to get her dressed for a day of hanging out at the mall or lounging in front of the TV. She may be a star, but she denies that she dresses like a celebrity. Vanessa does describe her style as bohemian and definitely funky. 'I just like putting things together myself,' she told *Life Story*. 'I like funky, vintage-looking, very unique clothing. I shop all over the place; if I find something fun and funky, I buy it.'

At the *High School Musical* DVD premiere, she looked super cute in a floral Betsey Johnson sundress, big gold heart necklace and gorgeous make-up. That outfit reflected her laidback style. She loves to mix it up. Sometimes she'll bedazzle her loungewear by donning a pair of sparkly sweatpants. Vanessa's also addicted to Frankie B jeans and has a closet (or two) filled with them. But to create her eclectic look, she loves to shop at a store popular with lots of kids her age. She told *Twist*, 'I'll buy just about anything from Urban Outfitters.'

Still, Vanessa is a big star with a big bank account. So sometimes she pushes past ordinary shops like Urban

Outfitters and goes for super high style. Her first major purchase after she gained some success was a limited edition Dior purse that she bought while in London. Chic and timeless, the bag is a perfect item on which to splurge. But she didn't stop there. While in Pittsburgh, of all places, she plunked down a wad of cash for a Chanel ring. Well, if anyone has earned a Chanel ring, it's Vanessa.

chapter 15

A Star's Bright Future

When Vanessa landed her first audition, she had no idea where that path would lead her. She's already achieved more than her wildest dreams. Vanessa's travelled all over the world, worked with talented producers and directors, made amazing friends, stretched herself to sing, and blossomed into a respectful, caring celebrity. And she's only at the beginning of her journey! Who knows how far she'll go?

Fame has brought recognition wherever she goes. Whether it's in an audition or simply on the streets, people know who Vanessa is before she has a chance to get to know them. That can be a challenge, but this star gets a major kick out of her public status. 'I think it's fun. How many kids get recognized?' she told *Life Story*. 'It's so inspirational, too, because there are these little four- or five-year-olds coming up to me and talking to me . . . and e-mails from people saying that I'm their inspiration and I give them hope.'

Despite how much her life has changed, Vanessa insists that she's still the same girl who loved to perform in local musicals at little venues. In fact, she says none of her *High School Musical* co-stars have been altered by their fame. 'We're the same people,' she told the *Cleveland Plain Dealer*. 'We're normal people. Except we recently have been getting busier.'

Not that Vanessa's complaining about being busy. She knows how fortunate she is to have a full schedule. She counts her blessings and doesn't assume it's a given that she will continue to get acting parts. As she puts it in *Life Story*: 'It's just a great personal accomplishment, and being recognized isn't going to last forever, so I may as well enjoy it as long as I can.'

If the critics have anything to say about it, Vanessa will be working for a long, long time. Even among the talented *High School Musical* gang, she stands out. 'The cast is destined for stardom, especially [Zac] Efron and [Vanessa] Hudgens,' *The Tampa Tribune* wrote. 'Hudgens is every bit as appealing as Lindsey Lohan or Hilary Duff, and she comes without tabloid baggage.' That's so true!

Vanessa still has more goals she would like to accomplish in her acting career. She dreams of one day working with adult superstars on meaningful projects. She would love to meet Angelina Jolie and work with Nicole Kidman. On the music front, she's a big fan of Christina Aguilera. 'My passion is doing movies, so as long as I keep doing that I will be happy,' she told *Scholastic News Online*. 'I want to be able to tackle good movies, fun roles and dramatic things. I love all of it, so as long as I continue doing it, I will be more than happy.' And as long as she's acting and singing, her fans will be happy, too.

With her great success comes great responsibility. It wasn't easy for Vanessa to deal with the fact that now she's a role model for kids all over the world. But she's ready to tackle her obligations to those who look up to her – just like she's tackled acting and singing. Her number-one piece of advice is to listen to your heart. Trust and believe in yourself, no matter what anyone else says. 'Follow your heart, because sometimes, I'll be torn between my head and my heart,' she revealed to TeenMusic.com. 'Sometimes, I'll think, "Well I'm not doing anything so I may as well go out for this", like as a career choice and it's turned out to be wrong. So I think you really have to go with your gut feeling.' Spoken like a true star.

chapter 16
Fast Facts Quiz

So you're Vanessa's biggest fan, but do you know everything there is to know about the *HSM* cutie? It's quiz time – and no skipping to the end for the answers!

1. **What is the name of Vanessa's pet pooch?**
   a. Dreamer
   b Shadow
   c. Dancer

2. **Which sweet snack does Vanessa admit she's totally addicted to?**
   a. Chocolate
   b Ice Cream
   c. Cupcakes

3. **What is the name of Vanessa's little sister?**

    a. Stella

    b Ashley

    c. Lauren

4. **Can you remember Vanessa's star sign?**

    a. Sagittarius

    b. Virgo

    c. Gemini

5. **What was the title of Vanessa's debut album?**

    a. *Viva*

    b *V*

    c. *View*

6. **Vanessa chose a song called 'Low' as her audition song for *High School Musical*. Do you know which star originally sang it?**

    a. Kelly Clarkson

    b Britney Spears

    c. Jennifer Lopez

7. **Which record label is Vanessa signed to?**

   a. Hollywood Records

   b. Sony

   c. Island Records

8. **On which TV show did Vanessa sometimes appear as Corrie, alongside her best friend Ashley Tisdale?**

   a. *Hannah Montana*

   b *Zoey 101*

   c. *The Suite Life of Zack & Cody*

9. **Who does Vanessa say are her musical inspirations?**

   a. Alicia Keys

   b Celine Dion

   c. Both of the above

10. **Which vegetable can Vanessa, really, really not stand?**

   a. Spinach

   b. Carrots

   c. Sprouts

Answers: 1. b, 2. a, 3. a, 4. a, 5. b, 6. a, 7. a, 8. c, 9. c, 10. b

chapter 17
Web Resources

Vanessa's life is always changing. Look how much has happened to her in just a few years. Seriously, this is one girl on the go. Now that she's been in one of the biggest television movies of all time and cut her own record, who knows what's next? A clothing line or maybe a hot new boyfriend? Or what about a major motion-picture deal? Vanessa is up for any challenge or adventure. Whatever this rising star takes on, you'll want to know all about it. So to keep up with the latest in her life, here is a list of websites for ongoing updates about Vanessa:

vanessaannehudgens.net

(A fan site devoted to Vanessa – this has updates of all her performances, appearances, and projects.)

imdb.com/name/nm1227814

(The Internet Movie Database has industry information
on all of Vanessa's work.)

en.wikipedia.org/wiki/Vanessa_Anne_Hudgens

(This user-driven encyclopedia provides biographical
information and fun facts about Vanessa.)

tv.com/vanessa-anne-hudgens/person/161961/

summary.html

(TV.com has anything and everything you
would want to know about Vanessa's TV career
and all the shows on which she's appeared.)

hsmusical.org

(This is a fan site devoted to *High School Musical*.)